JUDGE JUDY

REBECCA FELIX

**Checkerboard
Library**

An Imprint of Abdo Publishing
abdobooks.com

ABDOBOOKS.COM

Published by Abdo Publishing, a division of ABDO, PO Box 398166, Minneapolis, Minnesota 55439.
Copyright © 2020 by Abdo Consulting Group, Inc. International copyrights reserved in all countries.
No part of this book may be reproduced in any form without written permission from the publisher.
Checkerboard Library™ is a trademark and logo of Abdo Publishing.

Printed in the United States of America, North Mankato, Minnesota
052019
092019

Design and Production: Mighty Media, Inc.
Editor: Megan Borgert-Spaniol
Cover Photograph: Shutterstock Images
Interior Photographs: AP Images, p. 25; Everett Collection, pp. 5, 15, 17, 21, 29 (top right); Seth Poppel/
Yearbook Library, pp. 7, 28 (left); Shutterstock Images, pp. 10, 11, 19, 23, 27, 28 (top right, bottom right),
29 (left, bottom right); Susan Roberts/Wikimedia Commons, p. 13; Wikimedia Commons, p. 9

Library of Congress Control Number: 2018966242

Publisher's Cataloging-in-Publication Data
Names: Felix, Rebecca, author.
Title: Judge Judy / by Rebecca Felix
Description: Minneapolis, Minnesota : Abdo Publishing, 2020 | Series: Checkerboard biographies |
    Includes online resources and index.
Identifiers: ISBN 9781532119378 (lib. bdg.) | ISBN 9781532173837 (ebook)
Subjects: LCSH: Judge Judy (Judy Sheindlin), 1942- --Juvenile literature. | Courtroom drama--Juvenile
    literature. | Television personalities--United States--Biography--Juvenile literature. | Television
    programs--Juvenile literature.
Classification: DDC 791.4575 [B]--dc23

CONTENTS

CHAPTER 1

QUEEN OF COURT

Judith Sheindlin is best known by her nickname, "Judge Judy." Sheindlin has starred in a TV court program of the same name for more than 20 years. *Judge Judy* first aired in the 1990s. Since then, it has been the nation's most-watched daytime show. Millions of people tune in to watch Sheindlin in action each day.

But Sheindlin is not an actress. She is a real judge who had years of experience before appearing on TV. In her lifetime, Sheindlin has worked on thousands of cases.

Judge Judy is not the only court show on TV. But Sheindlin's attitude has made it the most successful. She is known for being tough and outspoken. But she is also known for her sharp sense of humor. Her remarks often leave people speechless.

> **Of course I'm right. I'm always right. I'm like a truth machine.**

Many people admire Sheindlin's courtroom style. Others think she is rude or too harsh. But no matter people's opinions of Sheindlin, *Judge Judy* has become an icon.

Sheindlin has a Guinness World Record for the longest career as a TV court judge!

CHAPTER 2

TALENT FOR TALKING

Judith Susan Blum was born in New York City, New York, on October 21, 1942. She went by Judy. Judy's father, Murray, was a dentist. Her mother, Ethel, took care of the Blum household and children. Judy has one brother, David. He is five years younger than Judy.

Judy's parents set a good example for their children. They raised Judy to have a strong moral compass. Judy's father also passed down his talents for comedic timing and storytelling. These inherited **traits** would serve Judy well in her future career.

Murray thought his daughter would become a politician. This was because Judy liked to argue and **debate**, as politicians often do. Judy was also smart and talkative. In fact, Judy realized talking was one of her greatest talents.

 It was a good kind of upbringing. It gave me a confidence, and ... that's the best gift you can give a child.

Judy decided her talent for talking and arguing would make her a good lawyer. She was

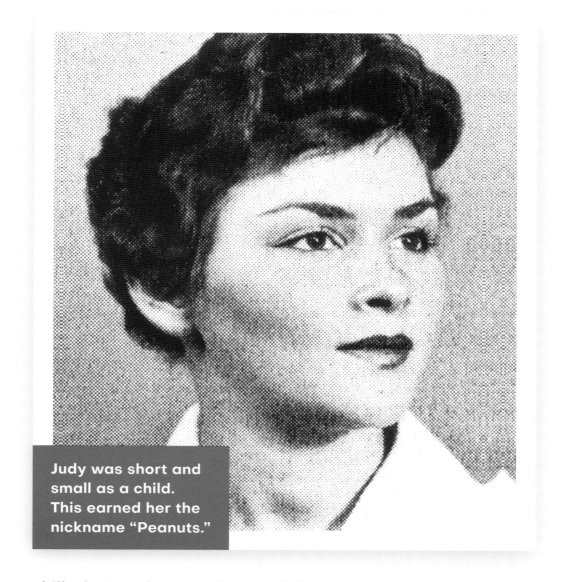

Judy was short and small as a child. This earned her the nickname "Peanuts."

skilled at understanding social situations and people. She believed these **traits** would benefit a career in law.

CHAPTER 3

SCHOOL & FAMILY

Judy needed more than a talent for talking and arguing to become a lawyer. She also needed an education. As a teenager, Judy attended James Madison High School in New York City. She considered herself an average student. But Judy worked hard in school. In 1958, she graduated early at age 16!

After high school, Judy attended American University in Washington, DC. She earned a **bachelor's degree** from the school in 1963. She continued her schooling at the university's College of Law. Judy was the only woman in a class of 126 students.

In 1964, while still in college, Judy married a lawyer named Ronald Levy. Together, the two moved to New York City. Judy attended New York Law School, where she completed her law degree in 1965.

The final step to becoming a lawyer was passing the **bar exam**. Judy passed the New York bar exam and then got her first job in 1965. She worked as a **corporate** lawyer for a **cosmetics** company.

New York Law School is located in downtown Manhattan. Sheindlin was one of only five women in her class at the school.

However, Judy didn't like her job much. After nearly two years, she quit. By this time, she and Ronald had two children, Adam and Jamie. For the next few years, Judy focused on raising her children.

CHAPTER 4

FAMILY COURT

When Judy's children were young, she spent much of her time with them. But she wanted to stay mentally sharp and engaged with other adults too. So, Judy took classes at New York University one night a week.

Judy also attended some university events. At one event in 1972, she saw a friend from law school. The friend told Judy about a job opportunity working as a lawyer for the New York family court system.

The job interested Judy. She applied for and got the position! Judy became a **prosecutor**, arguing against people accused of crimes. These crimes included child **abuse**, **domestic violence**, and robbery.

Judy was a tough and stern prosecutor. She had strong opinions about what was right and wrong. She also believed people must be held responsible for their actions.

Judy worked hard as a lawyer. But she felt her husband viewed her job as a hobby and not a serious career. She resented this. In 1976, Judy divorced Ronald.

Judy and Jerry Sheindlin divorced in 1990 but then remarried a year later.

Soon after her divorce, Judy met and began dating Jerry Sheindlin. Jerry was also a lawyer, and later a judge. Judy and Jerry married in 1977. Judy changed her name to Judy Sheindlin. She also became stepmother to Jerry's three children from a previous marriage.

CHAPTER 5

STERN & SUCCESSFUL

Over the next few years, Sheindlin continued her work as a prosecutor. By 1982, her attitude earned her a reputation. Sheindlin was known as a no-nonsense lawyer who was intolerant of **deceit** and **arrogance**.

In 1982, New York City mayor Edward Koch promoted Sheindlin. She became a family court judge. She was one of the nation's first women to earn this title.

Sheindlin took her new role seriously, judging with the same stern style she had as a lawyer. She felt family court judges were often too **lenient**, especially with juveniles and first-time criminals. Sheindlin did not give lighter punishments because of age or lack of criminal history. She wanted to show the public that crimes come with consequences.

Sheindlin's tough manner earned her another promotion in 1986. She became **supervising** judge in the Manhattan division of the New York family court system. In this role, Sheindlin helped manage court cases, **budgets**, and more for the trial courts.

Sheindlin's signature look includes a lace collar on her robes. She has worn this type of collar since she became a judge.

CHAPTER 6

OPEN TO PRESS

By 1993, Sheindlin was often judging more than 50 court cases each day. She had also pioneered an "open court" policy. This meant she allowed members of the public and press to sit in the courtroom during her cases.

Sheindlin believed that closed courts led to bad judging and lawyering. Without public witnesses, courtroom professionals may not be held responsible for bad decisions or actions. Sheindlin believed lawyers and judges should be **scrutinized** so they do their jobs well.

Several reporters sat in on Sheindlin's cases. Heidi Evans, a reporter from the *Daily News,* was a frequent visitor. Sheindlin's ruling style and open court policy made an impression on Evans. The reporter told her husband, Josh Getlin, about Sheindlin.

Getlin was also a reporter. He worked for the *Los Angeles Times*. Getlin visited Sheindlin's courtroom to witness her in action. Getlin decided to write a profile of the no-nonsense judge. The resulting article changed the course of Sheindlin's life.

Before Sheindlin, open courtrooms were not common. Courtrooms were usually closed to the public.

CHAPTER 7

AMERICA'S TOUGHEST

The *Los Angeles Times* published Getlin's article about Sheindlin in February 1993. Getlin called her "tart, tough-talking, and hopelessly **blunt**." He also wrote that Sheindlin was firm yet fair and committed to making a difference in people's lives.

The article also revealed another side of Sheindlin. Getlin wrote that she often told jokes in the middle of court proceedings! He said Sheindlin sometimes sounded more like a comedian than a judge, making everyone in the courtroom laugh.

Getlin's article described Sheindlin as somewhat of a hero. But he also detailed disapproving reactions to her style. While many of Sheindlin's peers appreciated her toughness, others thought she was too harsh. Some even thought Sheindlin might lose her job because of how outspoken she was.

Sheindlin did not lose her job for being harsh. Instead, she became famous for it! Getlin's article earned Sheindlin an unofficial title as "America's Toughest Family Court Judge."

Sheindlin knows she's a tough judge. She says, "I don't mind getting my hands dirty and I don't mind getting to the truth of a situation."

The article also earned Sheindlin more media attention. People wanted to know more about the tough New York judge. Later in 1993, Sheindlin was invited to give an interview on the news television show *60 Minutes*.

Sheindlin's televised interview earned her further attention, this time from a literary agent. The agent believed Sheindlin had an interesting viewpoint on the family court system. She suggested Sheindlin write a book about it. Sheindlin agreed and got to work writing.

Sheindlin's *60 Minutes* interview also caught the interest of a TV producer named Sandi Spreckman. Spreckman was a former producer of *The People's Court.* This was a TV show featuring a real judge who ruled over real court cases. It aired from 1981 to 1993.

Spreckman wanted to produce another TV court show. And she felt Sheindlin would make a great star. So, Spreckman contacted Sheindlin. At the time, Sheindlin was still working as a judge. But she was interested in Spreckman's idea and thought seriously about it.

" I eat liars for breakfast. "

BIO BASICS

NAME: Judith Sheindlin

NICKNAME: Judge Judy

BIRTH: October 21, 1942, New York City, New York

SPOUSES: Ronald Levy (1964-1976); Jerry Sheindlin (1977-1990; 1991-present)

CHILDREN: Adam and Jamie (son and daughter); Nicole, Gregory, and Jonathan (stepdaughter and stepsons)

FAMOUS FOR: her role as an outspoken TV judge

ACHIEVEMENTS: served as a New York family court judge for more than ten years; starred on the TV court show *Judge Judy* for more than 20 years; earned several awards and honors from colleges, universities, and other organizations

CHAPTER 8

JUDGE JUDY

By 1996, Sheindlin had been in the family court system for more than 20 years. She had worked on more than 20,000 cases. Sheindlin felt ready for a new adventure. So, she retired from the family court system. The same year, she finished writing her book.

Sheindlin's first book was published in February 1996. It is called *Don't Pee on My Leg and Tell Me It's Raining.* This playful title suggests that a person should not lie, especially when it is obvious he or she is lying. In the book, Sheindlin shares her thoughts about the family court system.

Just months after Sheindlin's book came out, she achieved a new level of fame. Sheindlin had decided to pursue Spreckman's idea to star on a TV court show. On September 16, 1996, the first **episode** of *Judge Judy* aired nationally. Sheindlin had started a new, exciting chapter of her career.

HOT BENCH

At first, Sheindlin didn't like the name producers chose for her show. She wanted to name it *Hot Bench.*

Sheindlin was 54 years old when her TV show first aired.

Judge Judy was an instant hit! The show wasn't the first of its kind. But Sheindlin's personality made her show a success. Viewers liked her attitude. Sheindlin became as famous for her snappy remarks as she did for her tough rulings.

Sheindlin's memorable remarks are often the result of her getting angry when people lie to her. How can she tell when someone is being dishonest? Sheindlin's son Adam says his mom is able to sense dishonesty. But Sheindlin says **logic** is the key. "If it doesn't make sense, it's probably not true," she says.

Judge Judy is an **unscripted** show. However, Sheindlin prepares for each **episode** by reading about the cases. Information about most court cases is public by law.

Judge Judy researchers look up cases that sound interesting and contact those involved. Many people choose to be on the show because they receive up to $500 for doing so. The show also pays any fines Sheindlin determines the **defendants** must pay.

WORKING HOLIDAY

Judge Judy is taped in Los Angeles, California. Sheindlin visits the city two times a month for two or three days. During this time, she judges 10 to 12 cases a day to create a week's worth of *Judge Judy* episodes.

Petri Hawkins-Byrd was the court officer for Sheindlin in the Manhattan family court. Now, he is the court officer on *Judge Judy*. The show has made him famous!

CHAPTER 9

AUTHOR & ADVISER

Judge Judy continued to rise in popularity each year. By February 1999, it was the nation's number one **syndicated** show. By that summer, Sheindlin's show had about 7 million viewers each week!

In 1999, Sheindlin published her second book, *Beauty Fades, Dumb Is Forever.* The book became a best seller. In it, Sheindlin encourages readers to succeed in both their personal lives and their careers.

Sheindlin published several more books in the coming years. She also earned success as an adviser. In 2006, Sheindlin and her stepdaughter founded a women's organization. Her Honor Mentoring advises young women on how to succeed and be their best selves.

In 2012, Sheindlin launched a website to share advice with her fans. Whatwouldjudysay.com features a new topic each month. Topics include everything from saving money to social media. Sheindlin shares her opinions about these topics and answers questions users send in.

Sheindlin doesn't only give advice in books and on the internet. She has become a popular speaker at high school graduations across the country.

CHAPTER 10

COURT ICON

Sheindlin hasn't stopped coming up with new ideas. In 2015, she created *Hot Bench*. On this TV program, three judges hear a case at once and come to a ruling together. In 2017, Sheindlin created *iWitness*. The TV game show aired for six weeks. In it, contestants competed to recall information from images and videos they reviewed.

Of all her work in TV, Sheindlin's first show remains her greatest success. For more than 20 years, *Judge Judy* has been daytime television's number one court show. By 2018, the program had 10 million daily viewers!

Sheindlin knows not everyone admires her outspoken opinions. However, she says even people who feel this way still watch her show. True to Sheindlin's style, she says, "I like it a lot better if you like me. But if you don't like me and watch me every day, what's the difference?"

There's only one person who gets the last word, and that's me.

Sheindlin has had her own star on the Hollywood Walk of Fame since 2006. In 2013, she became the highest paid TV star in the US!

TIMELINE

1942
Judith Susan Blum is born in New York City, New York, on October 21. She goes by Judy.

1965
Judy earns a law degree from New York Law School and passes the New York bar exam.

1977
Judy marries Jerry Sheindlin. She takes his last name, becoming Judy Sheindlin.

1963
Judy earns a bachelor's degree from American University in Washington, DC. She enrolls in the university's College of Law.

1972
Judy takes a job as a prosecutor for the New York family court system.

1982

Sheindlin becomes a New York family court judge.

1996

The first episode of *Judge Judy* airs on September 16.

2018

About 10 million people watch *Judge Judy* each day.

1993

The *Los Angeles Times* publishes an article about Sheindlin in February. Later in the year, she appears in an interview for *60 Minutes*.

2012

Sheindlin launches the website whatwouldjudysay.com.

GLOSSARY

abuse—the mistreatment of someone or something, either physically or with words.

arrogance—the attitude of believing one is better, smarter, or more important than others.

bachelor's degree—a college degree usually earned after four years of study.

bar exam—a test taken by those who want to practice law.

blunt—speaking in a way that is direct or to the point.

budget—the amount of money a person, company, or other organization can spend in a certain period of time.

corporate—relating to a large business or organization made up of a group of people who have the legal right to act as one person.

cosmetics—beauty products, especially makeup.

debate—to argue publicly about a question or a topic.

deceit—the act of being dishonest or misleading.

defendant—a person who is being accused of a crime.

domestic violence—an act between members of a family or household that results in serious physical or emotional harm.

episode—one show in a television series.

lenient—kind, patient, or tolerant.

logic—the science dealing with rules of correct reasoning and proof by reasoning.

prosecutor—a lawyer who argues to convict the person on trial.

scrutinize—to examine closely or critically.

supervise—to watch over or take care of something.

syndicated—broadcasted on many different TV stations at the same time.

trait—a quality or feature.

unscripted—not following a script. A script is the written words and directions used to put on a play, movie, or television show.

ONLINE RESOURCES

Booklinks
NONFICTION NETWORK
FREE! ONLINE NONFICTION RESOURCES

To learn more about Judge Judy, please visit **abdobooklinks.com** or scan this QR code. These links are routinely monitored and updated to provide the most current information available.

INDEX